EXPRESS YOURSELF!

EXPRESS YOURSELF!

AN ENGLISH WRITING EXERCISES WORKBOOK

TERESITA A. CALANTAS

PARTRIDGE

You may contact the author through tcalantas@yahoo.com.

Print information available on the last page.

To order additional copies of this book, contact
Toll Free 800 101 2657 (Singapore)
Toll Free 1 800 81 7340 (Malaysia)
orders.singapore@partridgepublishing.com

www.partridgepublishing.com/singapore

Contents

CHAPTER EIGHT: My Future

FOREWORD

Designed specifically for the purpose of helping the first year students of the Faculty of Policy Studies in Nanzan University build their ability to better communicate in English, this workbook is another experimental effort of the author's continued research on the positive effects of writing activities in oral communication.

The activities and exercises in this workbook guide the students, step by step, towards better writing in English. Students are taught to connect phrases to form sentences, and to form paragraphs by grouping sentences according to ideas (Chapters 1, 2 and 3). It also shows them how to formulate ideas and organize these in the process of planning a composition (Chapters 4, 5 and 6). Next, it teaches them to put together paragraphs to form a composition (Chapter 7). Finally, this workbook invites the students to combine and apply everything they have learned about composition planning and writing as they discuss their plans for the future (Chapter 8).

On the whole, this book employs an experiential approach. It aims at making the students reflect and make use of their own experiences, and direct their minds towards the future.

FOREWORD

AUTHOR'S NOTE & ACKNOWLEGEMENTS

The book is largely a compilation of original teaching materials accumulated as supplementary exercises to textbooks used by the author during the first two years of teaching the Writing Course for beginner-level students. The book was designed for mid-beginners in a setting where English is taught as a Foreign Language. From the second year of use up to this year, students who use the book were asked to evaluate the book's level of difficulty at the end of the semester. This revised edition includes some changes in the format of exercises, as well as additional words, phrases, and explanation of tasks to be done, based on students' feedback gathered for several years. 'Express Yourself' is used as a textbook in the Writing Class of first year university students in the spring semester.

The aim of the book was to address an urgent need of giving students a tool to encourage recall and application of what they've learned in high school. The first edition of the book was hurriedly done due to lack of experience and time. It was mainly because of no experience on the part of the author that an acknowledgements page was not included. I would like to take this opportunity to express my sincere gratitude to the following.

To Professor Tamami Wada who unselfishly gave her time to write the Japanese meaning of words and phrases in the Glossary of the first edition. To Ms. Umida Ashurova and Ms. Reillne Ambion, who have dedicated countless hours of their time to read through the book and have given me valuable comments and recommendations. I would like also to thank the first year students of the Faculty of Policy Studies at Nanzan University for their cooperation in evaluating the book's level of difficulty after having used the book for one semester. To the teachers and their students of three public high schools in Iloilo, Philippines, who have used the book partially as supplementary material in their English Writing classes, thank you for letting me know of the book's usefulness. And last but not the least, to my sister Julia, and the people whose support both moral and technical were crucial in my finishing this revised edition. Thank you all very much.

Seto City, June 2016
T. A. C.

TO THE STUDENT

This workbook has been created for you. You will use this instead of a notebook for your writing exercises. The topics are about yourself, your likes and dislikes, what you can do, your ideas, your part-time job, your life as a student, persons you admire, and what you want to do in the future.

At the beginning of every chapter, there is a list of useful words and phrases. These words and phrases are used in the chapter. If you encounter an unfamiliar word or phrase, check it out at the Glossary starting from page 119. The exercises are aimed to help you develop your writing skills. Each chapter ends with an Evaluation. After the Evaluation, is a Free-Writing Exercise that will earn you Bonus Points. This means that you don't have to do the Free-Writing Exercise, but if you do, you will be given extra points.

At the end of the semester, you are to submit this workbook for grading. You will be given points for the number of exercises that you have worked on. Your mistakes shall be corrected, but they will not be counted as minus points. Thus, the more exercises you do, the more points you will have. Good luck and happy writing!

-- T. A. Calantas

CHAPTER ONE

MYSELF

Skill: Writing Phrases

WORDS AND PHRASES

advertisement

arrange

at the same time

background music

backpack

compose

costumes

cultures

describe

ethnic

family members

interests

lodge

passage

phrase

religious festivals

remaining

scary

stuffed toy animals

to collect

trading company

varied

with a lot of muscles

works at

works for

My name is Megumi Kato. Learn more about me! Quickly read the passage below without using your dictionary.

> I was born in Shizuoka but now I live in Naka-ku, Nagoya City. My birthday is May 19th. There are five people in my family. I have an older brother and a younger sister. My brother is a medical student at a university in Tokyo, and my sister is a junior high school student. My father works for a big trading company, while my mother composes background music for advertisements on TV.

ACTIVITY 1: Completing Phrases

What to do:

Tell me what you learned about me by filling in the blanks to complete the **phrases** below.

1. Born___*in Shizuoka*_____

2. Live _____

3. Birthday is _____

4. Five people_____

5. Older_____at a University in Tokyo

6. _____sister in junior high school

7. Father works for a _____

8. Mother _____
   _____

YOUR SCORE: / 8   ★ 👍 ☺ 😐

> ## GRAMMAR CORNER
> **Phrase:** a group of related words that express a thought or idea

Quickly read the passage below to learn more about me.

> I have lots of hobbies. I like collecting stuffed toy animals, so my room is full of them. I bought some of them myself, but most were given by my friends and family members. I also like reading novels, watching movies, listening to music, and sometimes playing tennis.
>
> My interests are varied. I am very interested in people and different cultures, especially ethnic food, national costumes, and religious festivals. I also like attending parties and making new friends.

ACTIVITY 2: Copying Phrases

What to do:

From the passage above, look for hobbies and interests and write them on the blanks below.

MY HOBBIES

1. *collecting stuffed toy animals*

2. _____

3. _____

4. _____

5. _____

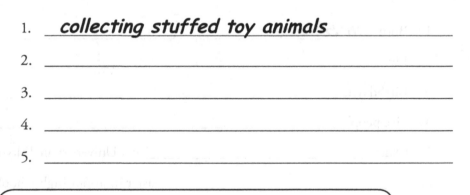

GRAMMAR CORNER

Past Participle: a verb in the past tense that can act as an adjective
- The toys were <u>given</u> by my friends.

Gerund (VERB + ing): a verb that can act as a noun
- I like <u>collecting</u> stuffed toy animals.
- You like <u>watching</u> movies.
- She likes <u>meeting</u> friends.

MY INTERESTS

1. ___*different people and their culture*___
2. _____
3. _____
4. _____
5. _____
6. _____

YOUR SCORE: / 9   ★ 👍 ☺ ☹

I also like to travel abroad and within Japan. Read the passage below to find more information

---

When I was a junior high school student, I went to South Korea on a school trip. Then, in high school I went on a 'backpack' trip to Sweden on my own. It was scary and hard, but was a great and memorable experience.

This summer, I plan to make a trip to Hokkaido. I don't have much money, so, I'm looking for a place through the Internet, where I can work and lodge at the same time. I am going to work for two to three weeks, and then use the remaining days of summer holidays travelling around Hokkaido.

ACTIVITY 3: Classifying Phrases (I)

<u>What to do:</u>

Write on the blanks below the things I have done and the things I plan to do. <u>Copy the phrases only</u>, not sentences.

THINGS I HAVE DONE

1. <u>*went to South Korea on a school trip*</u>

2. <u> </u>

THINGS I WILL DO

1. <u>*make a trip to Hokkaido*</u>

2. <u> </u>

3. <u> </u>

4. <u> </u>

YOUR SCORE: / 4   ★   👍   ☺   ☹

ACTIVITY 4: Classifying Phrases (II)

What to do:

Look at the list of phrases below. They are phrases that describe people--what they look like, how they feel, and what they do. Copy the phrases under the categories to which they belong.

~~watch TV and videos~~	~~sad and lonely~~	play tennis
angry and surprised	very happy	a little afraid
read the newspaper	thin and tall	has long legs
~~with a lot of muscles~~	go to work	has red hair

WHAT PEOPLE LOOK LIKE

<u>*with a lot of muscles*</u>

<u> </u>

<u> </u>

<u> </u>

HOW PEOPLE FEEL

<u>**sad and lonely**</u>

_____

_____

_____

WHAT PEOPLE DO

<u>**watch TV and videos**</u>

_____

_____

_____

YOUR SCORE: / 9   ★   👍   ☺   😐

ACTIVITY 5: Reinforcing Phrase Patterns

<u>**What to do:**</u>

Arrange the group of words below to form phrases that tell about **what I like to do**. Write those phrases on the blanks given.

1. stuffed, collect, animals, toy

    <u>**collect stuffed toy animals**</u>

2. park, take, a, in, the, walk

    _____

3. cream, ice, eat

    _____

4. tennis, with, play, my, friends

_____

5. summer, next, to, Bali, travel

_____

6. draw, to, learn, how

_____

7. cultures, about, read, other

_____

8. movies, horror, watch

_____

9. sandals, new, a, buy, pair, of

_____

10. e-mails, write, friends, to, other, in, countries

_____

YOUR SCORE: / 9   ★ 👍 ☺ ☺

EVALUATION

What to do:

It's your turn to talk about yourself. Complete the lists below with phrases about yourself. Remember, use **phrases** only. No single words, nor sentences!

ABOUT MYSELF

MY BIRTH

1. _____

2. _____

3. _____

4. _____

5. _____

MY FAMILY

1. _____

2. _____

3. _____

4. _____

5. _____

MY INTERESTS

1. _____

2. _____

3. _____

4. _____

5. _____

MY HOBBIES

1. _____
2. _____
3. _____
4. _____
5. _____

MY PLANS FOR NEXT VACATION

1. _____
2. _____
3. _____
4. _____
5. _____

YOUR SCORE: */ 25*   ★   👍   ☺   ☹

Comments:

ABOUT MYSELF
(Megumi Kato)

My name is Megumi Kato. I was born in Shizuoka, but now I live in Naka-ku, Nagoya City. My birthday is May 19th. There are five members in my family. I have an older brother and a younger sister. My brother is a medical student at a university in Tokyo, and my sister is a junior high school student. My father works for a big trading company, while my mother composes background music for advertisements on TV.

I have lots of hobbies. I like collecting stuffed toy animals, so my room is full of them. I bought some of them myself, but most were given by my friends and family members. I also like reading novels, watching movies, listening to music, and sometimes playing tennis.

My interests are varied. I am very interested in people, and different cultures, especially ethnic food, national costumes, and religious festivals. I also like attending parties and making new friends. In addition, I like travelling. When I was a junior high school student, I went to South Korea on a school trip. Then, in high school I went on a 'back-pack' trip to Sweden on my own. It was scary and hard, but was a great and memorable experience.

This summer, I plan to make a trip to Hokkaido. I don't have much money, so I'm looking for a place through the Internet, where I can work and lodge at the same time. I'm going to work for two or three weeks, and then use the remaining days of summer holidays travelling around Hokkaido.

FREE-WRITING

Bonus Points: _____

What to do:

Read again the passages that Megumi Kato wrote about herself. Then, look at what you wrote in the Evaluation. Write about yourself like Megumi did. Connect your ideas and make them into sentences.

MYSELF

_____

_____

_____

_____

_____

_____

_____

_____

_____

_____

_____

_____

_____

CHAPTER TWO

MY LIKES AND DISLIKES

Skill: Writing Sentences

WORDS AND PHRASES

allergic	lousy	so much
awful	lovebird	strong
classical music	living things	tacos
comic books	Mexican dishes	terrible
cruel/ty	mild	war
disgusted	neutral	
divorce	outdoors	
don't care for	output	
don't mind	once in a while	
exclamation	painful	
fight	peace	
happily	prefer	
hate	provided	
hot and spicy	peace	
hurry	prefer	
include	quarrel	
indifferent	reason	
indoors	relax	
intensity	snowstorm	
jazz	someday	

Hi! I'm Elizabeth Perkins. You can call me Lizzy. Quickly read the passage below to know me better, but don't look at your dictionary.

I live in Colorado with my mother, two sisters, and a brother. My parents got divorced two years ago, but we still see our father sometimes.

I have many likes and dislikes. These could be strong, mild, or neutral. On the 'likes' side, there are things I love, really like, like a little, and don't mind. On the other hand, there are things I hate or can't stand, dislike, and things that I don't care for.

For example, I love listening to music. Although I don't mind jazz, classical music is what I really like. I also love animals. While I don't mind taking care of rabbits and lovebirds, cats and dogs are the animals I would love to have. As to food, I like Mexican dishes such as tacos, the same way I like hotdogs, hamburgers, and pizzas.

GRAMMAR CORNER

Sentence: a group of words containing a complete idea. It has at least one **subject** and one **verb**. It ends in a period (**.**), question mark (**?**), or exclamation point (**!**).

<u>**Don't**</u> and <u>**Doesn't**</u>:
I don't, you don't,
they don't, we don't,
she/he doesn't
it doesn't

ACTIVITY 1: Completing Sentences

<u>What to do:</u>

Complete the sentences below by copying from the passage you have just read.

<u>WHAT I LOVE</u>

1. I love *listening to music* _____

2. I love _____

3. I also love _____

<u>WHAT I LIKE</u>

1. I like _____

2. I like _____

3. I also like _____

<u>WHAT I DON'T MIND</u>

1. I don't mind _____

2. I don't mind _____

3. I also don't mind _____

YOUR SCORE: / 8   ★   👍   ☺   ☹

Now quickly read the passage below about the things I dislike. Do not use your dictionary.

There are some things that I don't care for, Comic books, for example. I don't hate nor dislike them. I just don't have any interest in them. I also don't care for chocolates. I like other kinds of sweets better.

And then, there are things that I don't like at all. For example, the memory of the day my parents got divorced. I also don't like to quarrel with my brother or my sisters. Lastly, I don't like to hurry all the time. So I organize my schedule with time to relax in between things to be done. By doing this, I have better output and can stay away from stress.

As to the things I hate, I can name three. I hate people who are cruel to other people and to animals. I hate snowstorms because they keep me indoors. I also hate war. I can't understand why people in the world fight so much. I hope that someday, all living things can live happily and peacefully on earth!

ACTIVITY 2: Answering with Sentences

What to do:

From the passage you read, look for the answers to the questions I will ask you about myself. Answer in complete sentences, and begin each sentence with the word **"You."**

1. How do I feel about comic books?

   You don't care for comic books.

2. How do I feel about chocolates?

   _____

3. How do I feel about the memory of my parents' divorce?

   _____

4. How do I feel about quarreling with my brother and sisters?

_____

5. How do I feel about hurrying all the time?

_____

6. How do I feel about people who are cruel?

_____

7. How do I feel about snowstorms?

_____

8. How do I feel about war?

_____

YOUR SCORE: / 7   ★   👍   ☺   ☹

┌─────────────────────────────────────┐
│   **GRAMMAR CORNER**   │
│ **Using Do and Does:**   │
│ I do, you do,   │
│ they do, we do   │
│ he/she does, it does   │
└─────────────────────────────────────┘

ACTIVITY 3: Interviewing

Look at the Like-Dislike Scale below. The feelings are listed according to **intensity--HOW STRONG or HOW MILD they are.**

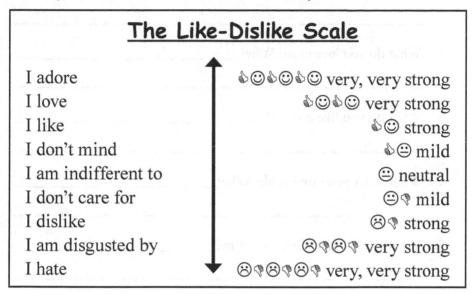

The Like-Dislike Scale

I adore	👍☺👍☺👍☺ very, very strong
I love	👍☺👍☺ very strong
I like	👍☺ strong
I don't mind	👍😐 mild
I am indifferent to	😐 neutral
I don't care for	😐👎 mild
I dislike	☹👎 strong
I am disgusted by	☹👎☹👎 very strong
I hate	☹👎☹👎☹👎 very, very strong

What to do:

Interview a partner about his/her likes and dislikes. Ask the questions on pages 23 and 24, and write your partner's answers in sentences. Remember to include the reason why.

Examples:
Who do you adore most? Why?
   I adore Beckham the most because he is handsome and a great soccer player.
What are you most disgusted by? Why?
   I am most disgusted by liars because they can't be trusted.

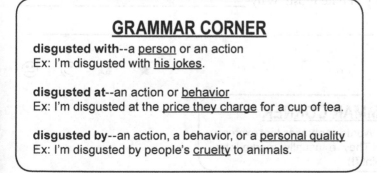

GRAMMAR CORNER

disgusted with--a <u>person</u> or an action
Ex: I'm disgusted with <u>his jokes</u>.

disgusted at--an action or <u>behavior</u>
Ex: I'm disgusted at the <u>price they charge</u> for a cup of tea.

disgusted by--an action, a behavior, or a <u>personal quality</u>
Ex: I'm disgusted by people's <u>cruelty</u> to animals.

NAME OF PARTNER: _____

1. Who do you adore most? Why?_____
   _____

2. What do you love most? Why?_____
   _____

3. What do you like most? Why?_____
   _____

4. What don't you mind at all? Why?_____
   _____

5. What are you indifferent to? Why?_____
   _____

6. What don't you care for most? Why?_____
   _____

7. What do you dislike most? Why?_____
   _____

8. What are you most disgusted by? Why?_____
   _____

9. What do you hate most? Why?_____
   _____

YOUR SCORE: / 9   ★   👍   ☺   ☹

┌───┐
| **GRAMMAR CORNER** |
| **Exclamations:** Words or phrases that express |
| strong feeling. They're usually marked by |
| exclamation point (!) |
└───┘

ACTIVITY 4: Classifying Exclamations

What to do:

Read the sentences below. Which sentences would mean "LIKE" or "DISLIKE"? Guess and write each sentence on the space provided.

<del>That's good!</del>   That's disgusting!

<del>It was terrible!</del>   I enjoyed every moment!

It was wonderful!   I never want to do this again!

This is awful!   I wish this never happened!

This is nice!   What a lousy day!

That's great!   Thank you so much!

LIKE

That's good!

_____

_____

_____

_____

_____

DISLIKE

It was terrible!

_____

_____

_____

_____

_____

YOUR SCORE: / 10   ★ 👍 ☺ ☹

EVALUATION

What to do:

Now it's my turn to ask you the questions that you asked your partner in Activity 3. Write your answers in complete sentences.

1. What do you love most? Why?

   _____

   _____

   _____

   _____

2. What do you like? Why?

   _____

   _____

   _____

   _____

3. What don't you mind? Why?

   _____

   _____

   _____

   _____

4. What don't you care for? Why?

   _____

   _____

   _____

   _____

5. What don't you like at all? Why?

_____

_____

_____

_____

6. What do you hate the most? Why?

_____

_____

_____

_____

YOUR SCORE: */ 24*   ★ 👍 ☺ 😐

Stu. No.: _____   Name: _____

MY LIKES AND DISLIKES
By Elizabeth Perkins

Hi! I'm Elizabeth Perkins. You can call me Lizzy. I live in Colorado with my mother, two sisters, and a brother. My parents got divorced two years ago, but we still see our father sometimes.

I have many likes and dislikes. These could be strong, mild, or neutral. On the 'likes' side, there are things I love, really like, like a little, and don't mind. On the other hand, there are things I hate or can't stand, dislike, and things I don't care for.

For example, I love listening to music. Although I don't mind jazz, classical music is what I really like. I also love animals. While I don't mind taking care of rabbits and lovebirds, cats and dogs are the pets I would love to have. As to food, I like Mexican dishes such as tacos, the same way I like hotdogs, hamburgers and pizzas.

There are some things I don't care for, Comic books, for example. I don't hate nor dislike them, I just don't have any interest in them. I also don't care for chocolates.

I like other kinds of sweets better.

And then, there are things that I don't like at all. For example, the memory of the day when my parents got divorced. I also don't like to quarrel with my brother or my sisters. Lastly, I don't like to hurry all the time. So, I organize my schedule with time to relax in between things to be done. By doing this, I have better output and can stay away from stress.

As to things I hate, I can name three. I hate people who are cruel to other people and to animals. I hate snowstorms because they keep me indoors. I also hate war. I can't understand why people in the world fight so much. I hope that someday, all living things can live happily and peacefully on earth!

FREE-WRITING

What to do:

Read again the complete passage written by Elizabeth about herself. Then, write about your own likes and dislikes using the sentences that you wrote in the Evaluation (pp. 25-26). Group all your 'likes' sentences according to intensity. Do the same with your 'dislikes' sentences.

MY LIKES AND DISLIKES

_____

_____

_____

_____

_____

_____

_____

_____

_____

_____

_____

_____

_____

CHAPTER THREE

WHAT I CAN DO

Skill: Writing Paragraphs

WORDS AND PHRASES

ability	Naples
boast	note down
by the sea	note-taking
clan	often
commercial plane	perform
compare	performance tour
expert	prepare dinner
flying school	pretend
go out to sea	relatives
indent	secrets
indention	support
interview	technique
licensed	troupe
light plane	unbeatable
main idea	woodwind

Hello! My name's Gaspare Ligouri. I live in Italy, in the city of Naples. Read quickly the passage below without looking at your dictionary.

> <u>I come from a big family.</u> The members of my family are: my mother, my father, three sisters, two brothers, and myself. I have many uncles, aunts and cousins. I also have grandparents, granduncles and grandaunts. During certain holidays, we all come together as a clan to eat, dance, sing, and have fun.

What you just read is a **paragraph.**
The underlined sentence is the **topic sentence.**
The other sentences are called **supporting sentences.**

PARAGRAPH=Topic sentence   +   **Supporting sentences**

It tells us the main idea of the paragraph.   *They add information*
It may be found at the BEGINNING,   *about the topic sentence.*
MIDDLE or END of the paragraph.

ACTIVITY 1: Finding Topic Sentences

<u>**What to do:**</u>

Look for the topic sentence in each paragraph and <u>underline</u> it. Paragraph 1 has been answered for you.

1) <u>Because Naples is by the sea, many of the men in our clan are fishermen.</u> My father is a fisherman. My uncles are fishermen. Their fathers were fishermen, too. My cousins and I are training to be fishermen. Someday our sons, too, will go out to sea and catch fish.

2) My younger brothers already know how to catch fish. They can do it well, but I can catch fish better. That's because I am older and have been out to sea more. Yet my father can catch fish better than I can. He knows many techniques that I still have to learn. However, in our family, it is my grandfather who is the best in catching fish.

3) While my grandfather is the best fisherman in the clan, it is my grandmother who is the best cook. She knows many ways of cooking fish. She would boil, steam, fry, or bake them, prepare them with vegetables, or put them on pasta. When my grandmother prepares a dish, it is always delicious.

4) My sisters are learning how to cook. My mother teaches them. Every Saturday afternoon, they go to the kitchen to help her prepare dinner. Mother shows them different ways of preparing food. Through this, my sisters hope to learn the secrets of good cooking.

5) I know how to cook a little, but I can catch fish better than I can cook. I can't boast of my cooking nor my ability to catch fish. Yet, there is one thing that I am unbeatable at, and that is singing. I have a very good voice and no one among my relatives can sing better than I can. In our clan, there are many expert fishermen and excellent cooks, but I am the only singer!

YOUR SCORE: */ 4*   ★ 👍 ☺ ☹

ACTIVITY 2: Building Paragraphs from a Topic Sentence

What to do:

A paragraph can begin with a topic sentence which is followed by supporting sentences. For each topic sentence below, add 3-5 supporting sentences. For number 1, a sample supporting sentence has been added.

1. *I have many good friends, but there is one whom I like best. Her name is Mika Kondo.*

_____

_____

_____

_____

_____

2. *I saw a movie that I really enjoyed.*

_____

_____

_____

_____

_____

3. *Among the dishes that I like, Japanese food is my favorite.*

_____

_____

_____

_____

_____

_____

YOUR SCORE: / 3   ★ 👍 ☺ ☹

ACTIVITY 3: Arranging Sentences to Form a Paragraph

<u>What to do:</u>

The sentences in the box are supporting sentences. For each number, the **topic sentence** has been provided. Arrange the supporting sentences in the order you think is best to form a paragraph.

There are many possible ways, so do not worry about making mistakes in arranging the sentences! Number 1 has already been done for you.

> When Vito plays the piano, everyone stops to listen.
> But he is even better on the piano.
> He also knows a lot of woodwind music.
> He can play the guitar very well.

1. **My friend Vito is a good musician.** He can play the guitar very well. He also knows a lot of woodwind music. But he is even better on the piano. When Vito plays the piano, everyone stops to listen.

> She travels around the world to perform.
> She performs with the country's top ballet troupe.
> Carla has been to Europe, Asia, Africa, and America.
> Because of her performance tours, Carla is now famous around the world.

2. **Carla is a wonderful ballet dancer.**

_____

_____

_____

> On her free days, Kika often flies her own light plane.
> She read books about airplanes and flying.
> When she grew older, Francesca went to a flying school to become a pilot.
> Kika, as she is commonly called, liked looking at airplanes.
> Now, she is a licensed pilot and flies a commercial plane three times a week.

3. *Even when Francesca was still a child, she already wanted to be a pilot.*

_____

_____

_____

YOUR SCORE: */ 8*   ★ 👍 ☺ ☹

```
┌─────────────────────────────────────────────┐
│          ★ Organizing Your Thoughts ★        │
│                                               │
│   1.  List all the ideas you want to include  │
│                                               │
│   2.  Group the ideas and remove ideas that   │
│       don't belong.                           │
│                                               │
│   3.  Form ideas into sentences.              │
│                                               │
│   4.  Study the sentences, and then, write a  │
│       sentence summarizing the ideas.         │
│           This is your topic sentence.        │
│                                               │
│   5.  Put the topic sentence at the beginning │
│       of the paragraph.                       │
│                                               │
└─────────────────────────────────────────────┘
```

EVALUATION

What to do:

Interview a partner. Find out what he/she does well, does better, and does best. Note down what your partner said. Then, write paragraphs about what your partner can do. Before writing, plan your topic sentences and supporting sentences.

_____

(My Partner's Name)

WHAT MY PARTNER DOES WELL

Take down notes:

Write a paragraph:

_____

_____

_____

_____

WHAT MY PARTNER DOES BETTER

Take down notes:

Write a paragraph:

_____

_____

_____

_____

WHAT MY PARTNER DOES BEST

Take down notes:

Write a paragraph:

_____

_____

_____

_____

YOUR SCORE: / 3   ★   👍   ☺   ☺

┌───┐

GRAMMAR CORNER

Do and **Does**:
I do, you do, we do, they do
he does, she does, it (my cat/ dog) does

└───┘

Stu. No.: _____ **Name:** _____

FREE-WRITING

<u>**What to do:**</u>

Pretend you are a famous person and that people want to know all about you. They want you to answer three important questions:

(1) **What can you do well?** (2) **What can you do better?** (3) **What can you do best?** Answer each question with a paragraph. As you begin each paragraph, don't forget to indent. Below are some ideas you might want to use.

Example: *Can do well—speak to people, singing, drawing, designing clothes*
Example: *Can do better—read aloud, listen, observing, communicating my ideas,*
                                meeting new friends, growing plants
Example: *Can do best—cooking, creating new dishes, planning, learning new*
                                things

WHAT I CAN DO

_____

_____

_____

_____

_____

_____

_____

_____

_____

_____

_____

CHAPTER FOUR

MY IDEAS

Skill: Finding Topics to Write About

WORDS AND PHRASES

additional	ideas	sky
alien	imaginary	smile
alone	in mind	Solar System
bright	interviewer	subject
category	invent	tear
chart	island	title
childhood	knife	volcano
choose/chose	living things	
collection	look up	
composition	man-made things	
connect	minutes	
curious	nature	
events	outer space	
experience	Pacific Ocean	
famous	planet	
fire	remind	
garbage	seconds	

This chapter will teach you how to look for ideas to be used in writing. It will prepare you for Chapters 5, 6, and 7.

HOW TO LOOK FOR IDEAS TO WRITE ABOUT

Technique No. 1: ASK QUESTIONS

Be curious. Learn to ask questions. From the questions that you ask, you will find something to write about. Ask WHAT, WHO, WHERE, WHEN, WHY, and HOW.

For Example:

> WHAT is the sun made of?
> WHO do I like to talk to most?
> WHERE do I go when I want to be alone?
> WHEN was the last time I looked up at the sky?
> WHY do we wear shoes?
> HOW did I sleep last night?

ACTIVITY 1: Forming Questions (I)

What to Do:

Get a timer and time yourself. Write down 4 additional questions for each set of blanks. See how fast you can go.

WHAT Total Time: _____ minutes:_____ seconds

What *are you going to do this summer?*_____

What_____

What_____

What_____

What_____

<u>**WHO**</u>   Total Time: _____ minutes:_____ seconds

Who *is the fastest runner in the world?*_____

Who_____

Who_____

Who_____

Who_____

<u>**WHERE**</u>   Total Time: _____ minutes:_____ seconds

Where *did you buy those nice shoes?*_____

Where_____

Where_____

Where_____

Where_____

<u>**WHEN**</u>   Total Time: _____ minutes:_____ seconds

When *is the best time to call you?*_____

When_____

When_____

When_____

When_____

Why ***do people get angry?***_____

Why_____

Why_____

Why_____

Why_____

HOW   Total Time: _____ minutes:_____ seconds

How ***can I speak English better?***

How_____

How_____

How_____

How_____

YOUR SCORE: */24*   ★   👍   ☺   ☹

ACTIVITY 2: Forming Questions (II)

What to do:

Pretend that you are an interviewer. Write down questions that you would ask the persons or objects below:

<u>YOURSELF</u>

What do you learn in your part-time job?

_____

_____

_____

<u>A FRIEND</u>

Do you have any plans on Sunday?

_____

_____

_____

A FAMOUS PERSON

Do you enjoy being famous?

_____

_____

_____

_____

AN ALIEN FROM OUTER SPACE

What do you eat on your planet?

_____

_____

_____

_____

_____

YOUR OWN FEET

Are you tired?

_____

_____

_____

_____

_____

YOUR SCORE: /25   ★   👍   ☺   ☺

Technique No. 2: INVENT TITLES FOR IMAGINARY COMPOSITIONS

Think of titles you would like to make. From these titles you will be able to find something to write about.

For Example:

Kinds of Food that I Really Like	Ways to Save Money
Five Things I Can't Live Without	My Favorite Movie
What the Moon is Made of	Two Very Good Friends

ACTIVITY 3: Getting Ideas from Titles

What to do:

Complete the possible titles below by adding words on the blanks.

Six Ways __*to Make Me Smile*_____

My Favorite_____

My_____

The Best_____

One Hundred_____

What to do:

Think of five titles for compositions and write them on the blanks below.

1. _____

2. _____

3. _____

4. _____

5. _____

YOUR SCORE: / 9   ★   👍   ☺   ☹

Technique No. 3: CONNECT IDEAS TO WORDS

Some words give us ideas to write about because they remind us of other things, of experiences, places, events, or of people we know. Look for words that give you strong feelings. Then, write down the ideas that enter your mind when you see those words.

For Example:

Word:	**CANDY**
Ideas in my mind:	**sweet...... bright colors... my childhood........ delicious**

ACTIVITY 4: Getting Ideas from Words

What to do:

Read each word on the next two pages and write the first 3 ideas that enter your mind when you read it. You can write words, phrases, or even sentences, on the blanks. Do the activity as quickly as you can.

FLOWERS

_____

_____

RAIN

_____

_____

KNIFE

_____

_____

SEA

_____

_____

STARS

_____

_____

TREES

_____

_____

GARBAGE

_____

_____

FIRE

_____

_____

GRANDFATHER

_____

_____

_____

TEARS

_____

_____

YOUR SCORE: */ 30*   ★   👍   ☺   ☹

Technique No. 4: MAKE A TOPIC-COLLECTION CHART

Make a chart with 5 topic categories: PEOPLE, OTHER LIVING THINGS AND THINGS IN NATURE, MAN-MADE THINGS, PLACES, and EVENTS AND ACTIVITIES. Then, fill up each category with topics in phrase or sentence (statement/question/exclamation) form.

For Example:

TOPIC-COLLECTION CHART

PEOPLE	*my younger brother* *my teacher* *Who is my best friend?*
OTHER LIVING THINGS and THINGS IN NATURE	*volcanoes in Asia* *lions and tigers* *the cherry tree*
MAN-MADE THINGS	*robot technology* *What is the fastest car?* *candies*
PLACES	*islands in the Pacific Ocean* *Hokkaido* *How can I fix my bedroom?*
EVENTS and ACTIVITIES	*New Year's Party!* *backpacking next summer* *My birthday*

ACTIVITY 5: Building Subject Awareness

What to do:

Do the same as the example above. Write two topics for composition for each category in the Topic-Collection Chart below.

TOPIC-COLLECTION CHART

PEOPLE
OTHER LIVING THINGS and THINGS IN NATURE
MAN-MADE THINGS
PLACES
EVENTS and ACTIVITIES

YOUR SCORE: */ 10*   ★ 👍 ☺ ☹

EVALUATION

What to do:

Think of 5 interesting questions and write them down. Then, turn those questions into titles for compositions. Follow the example below.

Examples:

Question:	Why do I like strawberries?
Title:	**Reasons Why I Like Strawberries** or **My Reasons for Liking Strawberries**
Question:	What is Global Warming?
Title:	**Cause and Effect of Global Warming**

QUESTION 1:_____

_____

TITLE FOR QUESTION 1:_____

QUESTION 2:_____

_____

TITLE FOR QUESTION 2:_____

QUESTION 3:_____

_____

TITLE FOR QUESTION 3:_____

QUESTION 4:_____

_____

TITLE FOR QUESTION 4:_____

QUESTION 5:_____

_____

TITLE FOR QUESTION 5:_____

YOUR SCORE: */ 10*   ★   👍   ☺   ☹

EVALUATION PART 2
Points _____

What to do:

Think of 20 words that bring ideas to your mind and make you think of topics for compositions. Write those 20 words on the boxes below. Do not use the words that were used in Activity 4: (FLOWERS, RAIN, KNIFE, SEA, STARS, TREES, GARBAGE, FIRE, GRANDFATHER, and TEARS.)

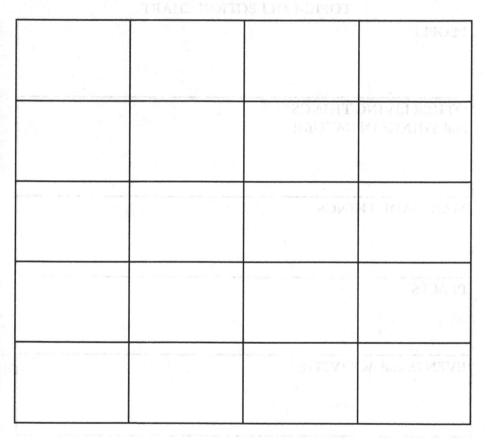

EVALUATION PART 3

Points _____

What to do:

Copy the **20 words from Part 2** and place each of them in the category to which they belong in the Topic-Collection Chart below. (Don't worry if one category has more words than the others!)

TOPIC-COLLECTION CHART

PEOPLE
OTHER LIVING THINGS **and THINGS IN NATURE**
MAN-MADE THINGS
PLACES
EVENTS and ACTIVITIES

YOUR SCORE: / 20   ★   👍   ☺   ☹

Stu. No.: _____ Name: _____

FREE-WRITING

What to do:

Look at the **20 words** that you wrote in the Topic-Collection Chart. From them, choose two words that you find most interesting. Copy those words on the space below. Then, write a composition about why each of the words is so interesting.

_____

(First Word)

_____

_____

_____

_____

_____

_____

_____

_____

_____

_____

_____

_____

_____

_____

_____

_____

_____

_____

_____

_____

                    _____

                    (Second Word)

_____

_____

_____

_____

_____

_____

_____

_____

CHAPTER FIVE

MY PART-TIME JOB (OR MY FAVORITE ACTIVITY)

Skill: Planning for a Composition

WORDS AND PHRASES

act

activity

cashier

change

contents

earn

entertain

fastfood

fill up

formulating

identity

par-time job

patient

planning

purpose

readers

responsible

restaurant

sheet

subtopic

school expenses

think

topic

tuition

$\mathbf{H}$i, I'm Hae Yeon Kim. I'm planning to write a **composition** about my part-time job here in Korea. Quickly read the **Planning Sheet** I filled up below.

PLANNING SHEET FOR A COMPOSITION

TOPIC (What do I want to write about?)

My part-time job.

PURPOSE (Why do I want to write about it?)

I want to tell readers about what I do, and why I enjoy doing it.

CONTENTS (What will I say about my topic?)

I am a cashier in a fastfood restaurant.

I work part-time so I can earn money for my school expenses/ my tuition.

My work is hard but enjoyable.

I have learned to work fast.

I have become more responsible.

I have learned to be patient.

I have made new friends.

I have met many nice people.

TITLE (What will I call my composition?)

Part-time Job can be Enjoyable

In Chapter 4, you learned to look for topics to write about. In this chapter, you will get some more practice.

ACTIVITY 1: Finding Topics for Compositions

What to do:

On the spaces below, write 3 topics that you can use for a composition.

TOPIC A

TOPIC B

TOPIC C

YOUR SCORE: / 3   ★ 👍 ☺ ☹

Next, think of **why** you want to write about the topics above. Ask yourself the following questions:

DO I WANT TO DESCRIBE SOMETHING TO MY READERS?

DO I WANT TO TEACH MY READERS SOMETHING?

DO I WANT TO TELL READERS HOW I FEEL?

DO I WANT TO CHANGE HOW MY READERS THINK AND ACT?

DO I WANT TO ENTERTAIN MY READERS?

ACTIVITY 2: Identifying the Purpose for Writing a Composition

What to do:

Give one purpose for writing a composition about Topic A, Topic B, and Topic C in Activity 1.

TOPIC A: PURPOSE
TOPIC B: PURPOSE
TOPIC C: PURPOSE

YOUR SCORE: / 3   ★ 👍 ☺ ☹

ACTIVITY 3: Formulating Subtopics

What to do:

Look at the example below. Then, go back to topics A, B, and C in Activity 1. Write 3 things you want to say about each of the topics. These are called **subtopics**. They can be written in phrase or sentence form.

Example:

Activity 1, TOPIC A: My Younger Brother

Activity 2, SUBTOPICS: **My younger brother's interests**
                                          My younger brother's favorite food
                                          My younger brother's hopes for the future

TOPIC A: SUBTOPICS

_____

_____

_____

TOPIC B: SUBTOPICS

_____

_____

_____

TOPIC C: SUBTOPICS

_____

_____

_____

YOUR SCORE: / 9   ★ 👍 ☺ ☹

A **title** is important. It is one way to make the reader curious about the composition. It should not be too long. It can be written in the form of a **phrase**, a **question** or an **exclamation**!

Examples:

What Is the Sun Made Of?
Memories of My Grandfather
What a wonderful view!

ACTIVITY 4: Writing Titles for Compositions

<u>What to do:</u>

Look at Topics A, B, and C again. Write a title for each of them on the spaces below.

TOPIC A: TITLE

_____

_____

TOPIC B: TITLE

_____

_____

TOPIC C: TITLE

_____

_____

YOUR SCORE: / 3   ★ 👍 ☺ ☹

EVALUATION

What to do:

Fill up the **planning sheet** below. Your topic will be about your **part-time job** or a **favorite activity.**

<u>TOPIC</u>
_____

<u>PURPOSE</u>
_____
_____

<u>CONTENTS</u>
_____
_____
_____
_____
_____
_____
_____

<u>TITLE</u>
_____

YOUR SCORE: / 7   ★   👍   ☺   😐

Stu. No.: _____ **Name:** _____

FREE-WRITING

What to do:

Write a composition about your part-time job or favorite activity. Use what you wrote in the **planning sheet** you filled up in the Evaluation.

_____

TITLE

_____

_____

_____

_____

_____

_____

_____

_____

_____

_____

_____

_____

_____

_____

_____

_____

_____

CHAPTER SIX

MY LIFE AS A STUDENT

Skill: Organizing Ideas Before Composition-Writing

WORDS AND PHRASES

anywhere	raft	at sea
assistant	refuse	first-aid kit
canoe	related	go for help
climb	route	Information Technology
compass	several	in the air
emergency	ship	main topic
extra	slippery	on land
flashlight	stress	proper attire
format	supply	safety tips
forecast	supply	take part
freshman	technology	taking up
glider	train	warm clothes
handle	transportation	
helicopter	truck	
items	unless	
jet	weather	
manage	whistle	
map	yacht	
organize		
outline		

Hello, my name's Vilma Patricio. I'm a freshman at Adamson University, taking up Information Technology. I'm writing a composition about **my life as student**. To do this, I must organize my ideas.

First, I will make a list of what I want to say. These will be the **main topics.**

   I. What I do in school
  II. How I manage my time   } **main topics**
 III. How I handle stress

Then, I will add ideas to support my main topics. These supporting ideas will be the **subtopics.**

  I. What I do in school
     A.   Study
     B.   Take part in club activities   } **subtopics**
     C.   Work part-time as student-assistant
 II. How I manage my time
     A.   Schedule my activities
     B.   Refuse extra work that I can't do   } **subtopics**
III. How I handle stress
     A.   Eat the right kind of food
     B.   Listen to music at home   } **subtopics**

The format I made above is called an **outline**. Making an outline is very useful when we want to write a composition. To know how to make an outline, you must practice doing it several times.

ACTIVITY 1: Organizing Main Topics and Subtopics

Part 1

<u>**What to do:**</u>

In the box below are some main topics and subtopics mixed together. Organize them into an outline by filling up the blanks with the items in the box.

Motorcycle	Glider	Jet
Hot-Air Balloon	On Land	Helicopter
Train	Truck	Yacht
Car	Raft	At Sea
~~In the Air~~	Ship	Canoe

KINDS OF TRANSPORTATION

I. *In the Air* _____

   A. _____

   B. _____

   C. _____

   D. _____

II. _____

   A. _____

   B. _____

   C. _____

   D. _____

III. _____

   A. _____

   B. _____

   C. _____

   D. _____

YOUR SCORE: _____ / 14   ★   👍   ☺   😐

Part 2

What to do:

Copy each subtopic below under the main topic it belongs to.

- ~~Wear proper attire warm clothes and boots that are not slippery~~
- ~~Never go anywhere alone~~
- Bring extra food
- Go back if the weather becomes bad
- Bring whistle, flashlight, and a first-aid kit
- Bring a map and compass
- Go back if there is a problem with the route
- Plan exactly where you are going to climb
- Always stay together--unless there is an emergency and someone has to go for help
- Do not change your route and schedule
- Check weather forecasts
- Tell other people where you will go and when you will return
- Know what to do in case of an emergency

SAFETY TIPS ON MOUNTAIN CLIMBING

I. **BEFORE MOUNTAIN CLIMBING**
    Subtopics:

- *Wear proper attire--warm clothes and boots that are not slippery*

_____

_____

_____

_____

_____

_____

_____

_____

_____

_____

_____

_____

II. **WHILE ON THE MOUNTAIN**
    Subtopics:

- *Never go anywhere alone*

_____

_____

_____

_____

_____

_____

_____

YOUR SCORE: */ 11*   ★ 👍 ☺ ☹

ACTIVITY 2: Completing Outlines

What to do:

Write your own subtopics on the blanks in the outlines on this page and the next.

THE THINGS WE WEAR

I. On the head

    A. _____

    B. _____

    C. _____

II. On the upper body

    A. _____

    B. _____

    C. _____

III. On the lower body

    A. _____

    B. _____

    C. _____

IV. On the feet

    A. _____

    B. _____

    C. _____

MYSELF, AT THIS MOMENT

I. What I am wearing

    A. _____

    B. _____

    C. _____

II. What I am doing

    A. _____

    B. _____

    C. _____

III. How I am feeling

    A. _____

    B. _____

    C. _____

IV. What I am planning to do later

    A. _____

    B. _____

    C. _____

YOUR SCORE: */ 24*   ★   👍   ☺   😐

ACTIVITY 3: Writing an Outline

What to do:

Fill up the blanks to make an outline on any topic you like.

_____

TITLE

I. _____

    A. _____

    B. _____

    C. _____

II. _____

    A. _____

    B. _____

    C. _____

III. _____

    A. _____

    B. _____

    C. _____

IV. _____

    A. _____

    B. _____

    C. _____

YOUR SCORE: / 17   ★   👍   ☺   😐

EVALUATION

What to do:

Make an outline about your own life as a student by supplying the subtopics.

MY LIFE AS A STUDENT

I.   What I do in school

    A. _____

    B. _____

    C. _____

    D. _____

II. How I manage my time

    A. _____

    B. _____

    C. _____

    D. _____

III. How I handle stress

    A. _____

    B. _____

    C. _____

    D. _____

YOUR SCORE: / 11   ★ 👍 ☺ ☹

Stu. No.: _____ **Name:** _____

FREE-WRITING

What to do:

Look at the outline you have made about your life as a student. Write sentences related to each subtopic. Arrange the sentences into paragraphs and write them on the space provided below under each subtopic.

MY LIFE AS A STUDENT

What I Do in School

_____

_____

_____

_____

_____

_____

_____

_____

_____

_____

_____

_____

_____

_____

_____

_____

_____

_____

_____

_____

_____

_____

_____

_____

_____

_____

_____

_____

_____

_____

How I Handle Stress

CHAPTER SEVEN

THE PERSON I ADMIRE MOST

Skill: Writing a Composition

WORDS AND PHRASES

admire	important	black people (blacks)
arrested	imprisoned	in danger
beliefs	injuries	no different
chained	inspiration	used to
cheat	joined	white people (whites)
contain	lie	
courage	martyr	
essay	organizations	
equal	principles	
equality	professions	
decide	relationships	
dedicated	respect	
deserve	rights	
fellow	rule	
formed	steal	
fought	stripped	
guide (v.)	summarize	
happening	tortured	
hero		

I am Louis Mthembu from Johannesburg, South Africa. I'm going to write a composition about the person I admire most. Quickly read the passage below without looking at your dictionary.

Parts of a Composition

BIKO: HERO AND MARTYR	Title
Stephen Bantu Biko is the person I admire most. He was born on December 18, 1946 in King William's Town, South Africa. When he was growing up, he learned that in his country, white people had a better life than black people.	Opening paragraph
Biko did not like what was happening to his fellow blacks. He decided to do something. He joined and formed organizations that fought for equality between black and white South Africans.	
Biko's actions made South Africa's white government very angry and he was arrested many times. On August 18, 1977, Biko was arrested for the last time. He was imprisoned, stripped of all his clothes, and chained. He was tortured by the police and died on September 12, 1977, because of head injuries.	Body
Because of the way he died, Biko became a martyr and a hero for the blacks of South Africa. He is remembered by everyone who believes that all people are equal, no matter what the color of their skin is.	Closing Paragraph

Please NOTE:

The **TITLE** is the name of a composition or an essay.

The **OPENING PARAGRAPH** or **Introduction** makes the reader curious and want to read more.

The **BODY** or **Content** contains the details about the subject matter.

The **CLOSING PARAGRAPH** or **Conclusion** summarizes the details in the Content and ends the composition.

ACTIVITY 1: Ordering Paragraphs in a Composition

What to do:

The paragraphs below have been mixed up. Read them and decide which paragraph comes first, which comes next, and which comes last. Put the words FIRST, SECOND, and THIRD on the blanks to the left of each paragraph. Then give the composition a title. (Examples: *My Hero* or *My Inspiration*)

_____
> Biko knew that the government didn't like his activities. He knew that his life was in danger. But he never stopped working for the good of his fellow black South Africans.

_____
> Biko died young, but he lives forever in the history of South Africa's black people. He is remembered by the world for his courage. Stephen Biko will always be my inspiration.

_____
> If there is someone in the world that I truly admire, it is Stephen Biko. Biko was a hero and a martyr to the black people of South Africa. He fought for their rights in a country where the white people used to rule.

_____
Title

YOUR SCORE: */ 3*   ★   👍   ☺   ☹

Read the passage below without looking at your dictionary.

MY GRANDFATHER

My grandfather is a man of principles. He has many beliefs which are important to him. They guide him in life. They help him in his relationships with people.

My grandfather believes that a man must be honest in everything that he does. He doesn't like people who lie or cheat. He doesn't like people who steal.

My grandfather also believes that a man with white skin is no different from a man with dark skin. He believes that a poor man deserves as much respect as a rich man does. My grandfather believes that all people are equal.

You have just read a composition I wrote about another person that I admire, my grandfather. How about you? Who are the people that you admire?

ACTIVITY 2: Composition-Writing from an Outline

<u>What to do:</u>

On the following pages, write a composition using the outline below to guide you. Write about people you know. Remember to indent the beginning of each paragraph.

THREE PEOPLE I ADMIRE

    A. Family Member or Relative
        1. Who is he/she?
        2. Why do I admire him/her?

    B. Someone in School
        1. Who is he/she?
        2. Why do I admire him/her?

    C. Someone at My Place of Work
        1. Who is he/she?
        2. Why do I admire him/her?

Examples:

A. My mother
    1. kind/ hard-working/excellent cook/fashionable
    2. she's a wonderful person

B. Mr. Koji Takeda
    1. Math teacher in high school/very interesting/dedicated to students
    2. very good person

C. Ms. Nana Sugiura
    1. kind and warm person/beautiful/serious/taught me a lot
    2. always willing to help others

_____

_____

_____

_____

_____

_____

_____

_____

_____

_____

_____

_____

_____

_____

_____

_____

_____

_____

_____

_____

_____

_____

_____

_____

_____

_____

_____

_____

_____

YOUR SCORE: */ 15*   ★ 👍 ☺ 😐

EVALUATION

What to do:

Interview a partner about himself/herself. Then ask your partner about his/her favorite person. Write a composition about your partner and the person he/she admires most. First make a simple outline. Let the outline guide and the example below show you how.

Outline Guide:

I.   My partner
   A. Who is he?
   B. What does he do?
   C. What is his personality?

II. The person my partner admires most
   A. Who does my partner admire most?
   B. What did this person do?
   C. What does my partner like about this person?

Example:

I. *Louis Gabriel Mthembu*
   A. *A student at a university*
   B. *He studies Art and works part-time at a restaurant*
   C. *A very intelligent and kind person*

II. *Stephen Biko*
   A. *A South African martyr*
   B. *Fought for the freedom of the blacks of South Africa*
   C. *Biko had courage and fought for his beliefs*

Write your QUESTIONS and NOTES in this box:

THE PERSON _____ ADMIRES MOST
(Partner's name)

My Partner_____

_____

_____

_____

_____

_____

_____

_____

_____

_____

_____

_____

_____

_____

_____

_____

_____

The Person My Partner Admires Most _____

_____

_____

_____

_____

_____

_____

_____

_____

_____

_____

_____

_____

_____

YOUR SCORE: */ 20*   ★   👍   ☺   😐

Stu. No.: _____ **Name:** _____

FREE-WRITING

What to do:

Write a composition about the person you admire most. Tell the reader about who that person is, what he/she does or did, and why you admire him/her. Give your composition a title.

_____

Title

_____

_____

_____

_____

_____

_____

_____

_____

_____

_____

_____

_____

_____

CHAPTER EIGHT

MY FUTURE

Free-Writing Supplement

CONGRATULATIONS!

You have reached the final chapter of this workbook and are now ready to go one step further.

Chapter Eight is all about writing a composition step by step, using what you've learned from the previous chapters. There is no doubt that this chapter is challenging, and so is the topic you will be writing about—**Your plans for the Future.**

But try it anyway and **have fun!**

In this chapter, you will write about what you wish to happen in the future.

ACTIVITY 1: Planning for a Composition

What to do:

Interview a partner about **3** of his/her plans for the future. Fill up the Planning List below.

TOPIC

**my partner's plans**

PURPOSE (see page 70)

CONTENTS (see pages 70-71)

TITLE

YOUR SCORE: / 5

ACTIVITY 2: Organizing for a Composition

What to do:

Make an outline of your partner's plans for the future using the planning sheet on Activity 1 as your guide. Use the example below to help you make your own outline.

Example:

TOSHIHIKO'S PLANS FOR THE FUTURE

    I. Toshihiko's plans
        A. First plan: to finish his college education
        B. Second plan: to get a good full-time job after college
        C. Third plan: to be a successful singer

    II. What Toshihiko will do to make his plans come true
        A. For the first plan: study well
        B. For the second plan: finish college
        C. For the third plan: take music lessons

Title
_____

I. _____

    A. _____

    B. _____

    C. _____

II. _____

    A. _____

    B. _____

    C. _____

YOUR SCORE: / 9   ★   👍   ☺   ☹

ACTIVITY 3: Writing the Composition

What to do: Write a composition about your partner's plans for the future. Use the outline you made in Activity 2 as a guide. Remember to indent the first line of every paragraph

Title

_____

_____

_____

_____

_____

_____

_____

_____

_____

_____

_____

_____

_____

YOUR SCORE: _/ 20_

★ 👍 ☺ 😐

EVALUATION

Points _____

What to do:

Fill up the planning sheet below. Let your topic be **your own plans for the future.**

Planning Sheet

TOPIC
My own plans for the future
PURPOSE
CONTENTS
TITLE

YOUR SCORE: / 5   ★   👍   ☺   😐

What to do:

Make an outline of your own plans for the future. Use the planning sheet you just made to guide you.

Title
_____

I. _____

    A. _____

       _____

    B. _____

       _____

    C. _____

       _____

II. _____

    A. _____

       _____

    B. _____

       _____

    C. _____

       _____

YOUR SCORE: / 9   ★   👍   ☺   ☹

Stu. No.: _____ **Name:** _____

FREE-WRITING

Bonus Points: _____

What to do:

Write a composition about your own plans for the future. Use the outline you made in the Evaluation as a guide. Remember to indent the first line of every paragraph.

_____

Title

_____

_____

_____

_____

_____

_____

_____

_____

_____

_____

_____

Symbols for Corrections

sp	spelling
wo	word order
ww	wrong word/ find and use another word
¶	start a new paragraph
→	indent
/	unnecessary / omit
?	idea not clear
~	exchange the order of words
RW	re-write

Symbols for Comments and Grade Equivalents

Excellent!	(100 points)	★
Good	(75 points)	👍
Satisfactory	(50 points)	☺
You can do better next time!	(less than 50 points)	☹

Glossary

A

ability *(n.)* 能力
act *(v.)* 実行する
activity *(n.)* 活動
additional *(adj.)* 追加の
admire *(v.)* 称賛する
advertisement *(n.)* 広告
alien *(n.)* 宇宙人
allergic *(adj.)* アレルギー (性) の
alone *(adj.)* 一人で
anywhere *(adv.)* どこへ (に) も
arrange *(v.)* 組み合わせる
arrest *(v.)* 逮捕する
assistant *(n.)* 助手
at the same time *(prep. phrase)* 同時に
at sea *(adj.)* 航海中で
awful *(adj.)* ひどい

B

backpack *(n.)* リュックサック
become/became *(v.)* ～の状態になる
beliefs *(n.)* 信念
black people (blacks) *(n. phrase)* 黒人
boast *(v.)* 〈自分が〉〈...だと〉自慢する
bright *(adj.)* あざやかな
by the sea *(adj. phrase)* 海のそばに [で]

C

canoe *(n.)*　カヌー

cashier *(n.)*　レジ係り

category *(n.)*　カテゴリー

chain *(v.)*　〜を束縛する

change *(v.)*　〜を変える

chart *(n.)*　図、表

cheat *(v.)*　〜をだます

childhood *(n.)*　子供時代

choose/chose *(v.)*　選ぶ・選んだ

clan *(n.)*　氏族、一家

classical music *(n. phrase)*　クラシック音楽

climb *(v.)*　登る

collect *(v.)*　集める

collection *(n.)*　収集

comic books *(n. phrase)*　漫画本

commercial plane *(n. phrase)*　商用飛行機

compare *(v.)*　比較する

compass *(n.)*　羅針盤、コンパス

compose *(v.)*　〜を構成する

composition *(n.)*　作文

connect *(v.)*　結びつける、 関係つける

contain *(v.)*　〈...を〉（内に）含む, 包含する

contents *(n.)*　内容

costumes *(n.)*　衣装

courage *(n.)*　勇気

cruel *(adj.)*　冷酷な

cruelty *(n.)*　冷酷さ

curious *(adj.)*　好奇心が強い

culture *(n.)*　（ある国・ある時代の）文化

D

decide *(v.)*　決心する、決める

dedicated *(adj.)* 専用な、熱心な
describe *(v.)* 描写する
deserve *(v.)* ～を受けるに足る
disgusted *(adj.)* うんざりした
divorce *(n.)* 離婚
don't care for *(v. phrase* ～が好きでない
don't mind *(v. phrase)* ～を気にしない

E

earn *(v.)* 稼ぐ
emergency *(n.)* 非常(緊急)事態
entertain *(v.)* ～を楽しませる
equal *(adj.)* 等しい
equality *(n.)* 平等
ethnic *(adj.)* 民族の
essay *(n.)* エッセイ, 文語
events *(n.)* 催し物
exclamation *(n.)* 感嘆
experience *(v.)* 経験する
expert *(adj.)* 専門家の
extra *(adj.)* 必要以上の

F

family memebers *(n.phrase)* 家族の一員
famous *(adj.)* 有名な
fastfood *(adj.)* ファ-ストフード
fellow *(adj.)* (blacks) 仲間の
fight *(v.)* 戦う
fill up *(v.phrase)* 記入する、書く
fire *(n.)* 火事
first-aid kit *(n. phrase)* 応急手当道具
flashlight *(n.)* 懐中電灯
flying school *(n. phrase)* 航空学校

forecast *(v.)* 　予想する

format *(v.)* 　形式を整える、フォーマットを整える

form *(v.)* 　形作る

formulate *(v.)* 　〈計画・意見などを〉組織立てる, まとめる

fought *(v.)* 　戦った

freshman *(n.)* 　1年生

G

garbage *(n.)* 　ごみ

glider *(n.)* 　グライダー

go for help *(v. phrase)* 　助けに行く

go out to sea *(v. phrase)* 　出航する

guide *(v.)* 　案内する

H

handle *(v.)* 　〜を扱う

happen/ing *(v.)* 　起こる

happily *(adv.)* 　楽しく

hate *(v.)* 　〜をひどく嫌う、憎む

health *(n.)* 　健康

helicopter *(n.)* 　ヘリコプター

hero *(n.)* 　英雄

hot and spicy *(adj. phrase)* 　ひりひりする, 辛い

hurry *(v.)* 　急ぐ

I

ideas *(n.)* 　考え

identify *(v.)* 　〜を確認する、思い出す

identity *(n.)* 　アイデンティティー

imaginary *(adj.)* 　想像上の

important *(adj.)* 　重要な

imprisoned *(v.)* 　刑務所に入れられた

include (v.)　含む

in danger (adj.)　危険な状態にある

indent (v.)　（章・節の一行目の頭の) 字を下げる

indention (n.)　（字下げの) 引っ込み スペース

indifferent (adj.)　無関心な

indoors (adv.)　屋内で

indifferent (adj.)　無関心な

information (n.)　情報

injury (n.)　怪我

in mind (adv. phrase)　私の考えでは

inspiration (n.)　霊感

intensity (n.)　激しいこと

interests (n.)　興味

interview (v.)　会見する, インタビュー

in the air (adj.)　広まって

invent (v.)　発明する

island (n.)　島

J

jazz (n.)　ジャズ

jet (n.)　ジェット機

join (v.)　活動などで 〈人に〉加わる

K

knife (n.)　ナイフ

L

lie (v.)　嘘をつく

light plane (n. phrase)　ライト プレイン （軽 飛行機 ）

licensed (adj.)　免許を受けた、許可された

living things (n. phrase)　生き物

lodge (n.)　山小屋

look up *(v. phrase)*　尊敬する
lousy *(adj.)*　汚い
lovebird *(n.)*　ボタンインコ

M

main idea *(n. phrase)*　主要な着想
main topic *(n. phrase)*　主題
man-made things *(n. phrase)*　人工のもの
manage *(v.)*　経営する
map *(n.)*　地図
martyr *(n.)*　殉職者
Mexican dishes *(n. phrase)*　メキシコ料理
mild *(adj.)*　軽い、マイルドな
minutes *(n.)*　議事録

N

Naples *(n.)*　ナポリ
nature *(n.)*　自然
neutral *(adj.)*　中立の
no different *(adj.)*　違うことなく
note down *(v. phrase)*　書き留める、聞きながら大事な点を書く
note-taking *(v. phrase)*　覚え書き, メモを書く

O

often *(adv.)*　しばしば, たびたび,よく
on land *(adj.)*　上陸して
once in a while *(adv. phrase)*　時々
organizations *(n.)*　組織
organize *(v.)*　組織化する
outdoors *(adv.)*　屋外で
outer space *(n. phrase)*　大気圏外空間
outline *(n.)*　外形

output *(v.)*　産出する

P

Pacific Ocean*(proper n.)*　太平洋
painful *(adj.)*　痛い
patient *(adj.)*　患者
passage *(n.)*　一節
peace *(n.)*　平和
perform *(v.)*　実行する
performance tour *(n. phrase)*　上演などのツアー ; パフォーマンスツアー
phrase *(n.)*　句
planet *(n.)*　惑星
plan *(v.)*　計画する
prefer *(v.)*　むしろ～のほうを好む
prepare dinner *(v. phrase)*　夕食の準備をする
pretend *(v.)*　ふりをする
principles *(n.)*　原則
professions *(n.)*　（専門知識必要とする) 職業
proper attire *(n. phrase)*　適切な服装
provide *(v.)*　供給する
purpose *(n.)*　目的

Q

quarrel *(v.)*　けんかする

R

raft *(n.)*　いかだ
readers *(n.)*　読者
reason *(n.)*　理由
refuse *(v.)*　拒否する
related *(adj.)*　関係のある
relationships *(n.)*　関係

relative *(n.)*　親類の人

relax *(v.)*　くつろぐ

religious festival *(n. phrase)*　宗教的な祝祭

remaining *(adj.)*　残った, 残りの

remind *(v.)*　気付かせる

respect *(n.)*　尊敬する

responsible *(adj.)*　責任がある

restaurant *(n.)*　レストラン

rights *(n.)*　権利

route *(n.)*　路線

rule *(v.)*　支配する

S

safety tips *(n. phrase)*　安全内報, 密告, 情報

scary *(adj.)*　恐ろしい

school expenses *(n. phrase)*　学費などの経費

seconds *(n.)*　秒

secrets *(n.)*　秘密

several *(indef det)*　いくつかの

sheet *(n.)*　刷り紙

ship *(n.)*　船

sky *(n.)*　空

slippery *(adj.)*　滑りやすい

smile *(n.)*　微笑

snowstorms *(n.)*　吹雪

so much *(adv. phrase)*　そんなに多くの

someday *(adv.)*　いつか

solar system *(n. phrase)*　太陽熱利用システム

steal *(v.)*　盗む

stress *(v.)*　〜を強調する

strip *(v.)*　人を〉裸にする

strong *(adj.)*　強い

stuffed toy animals *(n. phrase)*　ぬいぐるみ

subject *(n.)*　学科、科目

subtopic *(n.)*　副課題

summarize *(v.)*　要約する

supply *(v.)*　供給する

support *(v.)*　支える

T

tacos *(n.)*　タコス　《トルティーヤ に肉・チーズ・野菜などをくるんだメキシコ料理》

take part *(v. phrase)*　参加する

take up *(v. phrase)*　取り上げる, 従事する

teach *(v.)*　教える

tears *(n.)*　涙

technique *(n.)*　技術, 技巧, テクニック

technology *(n.)*　技術

terrible *(adj.)*　ひどい

think *(v.)*　考える

title *(n.)*　題名

topic *(n.)*　テーマ

torture *(v.)*　〜を拷問にかける

train *(n.)*　電車

trading company *(n. phrase)*　貿易会社

transportation *(n.)*　交通機関

troupe *(n.)*　一隊

truck *(n.)*　トラック

tuition *(n.)*　授業料

U

unbeatable *(adj.)*　太刀打ちできない

unless *(conj.)*　もし〜しなければ

used to *(v. phrase)*　…に慣れて

V

varied *(adj.)* 　様々な
volcano *(n.)* 　火山

W

war *(n.)* 　戦争
warm clothes *(n. phrase)* 　暖かい洋服
weather *(n.)* 　天気
whistle *(n.)* 　口笛
white people (whites) *(n. phrase)* 　白人
with a lot of muscles *(adj. phrase)* 　筋 (肉) の; 筋骨たくましい; 強い
woodwind *(n.)* 　(オーケストラの) 木管楽器
wonderful *(adj.)* 　素晴らしい
works at *(v. phrase)* 　…で 仕事している
works for *(v. phrase)* 　…のために働く

Y

yacht *(n.)* 　ヨット

Printed in the United States
by Bookmasters

Printed in the United States
By Bookmasters